HELP!

MY MONSTERS ARE
ON THE LOOSE!

i HAD FOURTEEN MONSTERS, NOW i HAVE NONE . . .

i LEFT THE WiNDOW OPEN, NOW THEY' VE ALL GONE !

FORGIVE ME FOR SUCH A SILLY
BLUNDER...

WHERE COULD THEY BE
i WONDER...?

HE'S RUNNING WILD
AND FREE.
PLEASE HELP ME FIND

TIMBURLY

HE'S NOT A CAT.
HE'S ALSO NOT A DOG.

CAN YOU SPOT
BABBLEBOG?

WHERE'S

WOMPUS

GOT TO?
CAN YOU HELP ME, BECAUSE i
HAVEN'T GOT A CLUE.

This is
Nitti

i think she's lost in the big city.

CAN YOU SPOT GERMY?

HE'S BEEN ON QUITE THE JOURNEY.

i've LOST

MiLLOY

SHE'S A GiRL, NOT A BOY.

SPABBLE LIKES TO HAVE FUN.
HE'S GOT A SPOTTY GREEN BODY AND A
BRIGHT RED TONGUE!

THANK YOU FOR HELPING, YOU'RE EVER SO KIND.

SEVEN MONSTERS FOUND, SEVEN LEFT TO FIND...

He's the same size as a poodle.
Have you seen

KADOODLE?

HELP ME FIND

GOOB

iF YOU WiLL.
HE'S GOT AN UNCLE NAMED PETRA
AND AN AUNTiE CALLED PHiL.

CAN YOU FIND McDIDDLE?
HE DOESN'T LIKE STANDING IN THE MIDDLE.

SHE'S VERY RARE.
HAVE YOU SEEN
EGGLES
ANYWHERE?

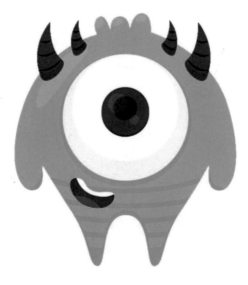

Can you find
GRUMP
for me?
He needs to come home for his tea.

i KNOW SHE MUST BE AROUND.
SO is
FLONKY
ANYWHERE TO BE FOUND?

i love my

WiNKYBOO

but where has she got to?

THANK YOU!

MY MONSTERS ARE FOUND!

NOW THEY'RE COMING
BACK HOME, ALL SAFE
AND SOUND.

71225329R00022

Made in the USA
Lexington, KY
18 November 2017